JOHN LENNON

PAUL McCARTNEY

Their Magic and Their Music

Bruce Glassman

B L A C K B I R C H   P R E S S
W O O D B R I D G E ,   C O N N E C T I C U T

Published by Blackbirch Press, Inc.
One Bradley Road
Woodbridge, CT 06525

© 1995 Blackbirch Press, Inc.
First Edition

Printed in Canada

10 9 8 7 6 5 4 3 2 1

Photo Credits

Library of Congress Cataloging-in-Publication Data
Glassman, Bruce.
  Lennon & McCartney : their magic and their music / by Bruce Glassman — 1st ed.
    p. cm. — (Partners II)
  Includes bibliographical references and index.
  ISBN 1-56711-135-1
  1. Lennon, John, 1940– —Juvenile literature. 2. McCartney, Paul—Juvenile literature. 3. Rock musicians—England—Biography—Juvenile literature. 4. Cooperation—Juvenile literature. [1. Lennon, John, 1940– . 2. McCartney, Paul. 3. Musicians. 4. Composers. 5. Rock music.]
I. Title. II. Title: Lennon and McCartney. III. Series
ML3930.L34G35 1995
782.42166'092'2—dc20
[B]   94-48459
                                         CIP
                                       MN AC

Table of Contents

John Lennon and Paul McCartney were the songwriting team that fueled the most popular group in music history.

When Opposites Attract

"The combination of John Lennon and

Paul McCartney, as friends as well as

songwriters, must rank as one of the great

examples of opposites being drawn

together like magnets."

—*Ray Coleman, from his
biography,* Lennon

There are dozens of popular theories about what the necessary ingredients are for a successful partnership. Many people argue that happy, long-term partners must have a great deal in common and must be "compatible" in key ways. Others believe that the most dynamic and creative partnerships are based upon the blending of two opposite personalities that complement one another. In the case of Paul McCartney and John Lennon, both these theories seem to apply, even though, on the outside, the two partners could not have been more different.

One thing Paul McCartney and John Lennon had in common was a passion for music. Without this interest to bring them together, however, the two probably would never have even met. In the most obvious ways, they were opposites: Paul was a well-behaved over-achiever who relished the approval of his elders. John was a rebel who sneered at conformity and hated being told what to do. Young Paul was an honor student who studied diligently and set a good example for his peers. John spent most of his school days on the verge of being expelled. Paul has always been an eternal optimist, relishing the romantic, sweet side of life. John never let the world please him too much, forever reveling in the macabre, the cruel, and the cynical.

Like all great creative partnerships or groups, each member has a specific part to play that is a unique contribution to the whole. For the most popular group in the history of popular music—the Beatles—the individual roles were typically compared to different parts of a living organism: John was commonly considered the brain, while Paul was the heart. George Harrison was the soul, and Ringo Starr provided the arms and legs that kept the body moving. Of course, none of these roles is better or more important than the other—all are required for a healthy, thriving organism. These body parts are only useful if they work together. The same truth applied to the Beatles. None of its members alone could have approached the level of creative genius or fame that they achieved together. Their solo careers after the Beatles years is a testament to that fact. Even Paul, who has maintained post-Beatles megastardom well into his fifties, has never been able to match the vitality or diversity of his Beatles days. Admittedly, he has had a number of great moments since going it alone, but his music has never approached the level of complexity or ingenuity that it had while he was composing with John Lennon. The same fate befell John during his ten solo years. As a solo artist, he achieved some notable success, but, on the whole, his songs lacked the structure, discipline, and softer perspective he gained from working with Paul McCartney.

Although the Beatles were pioneers in music, they were mimics as well. They began their careers by reinterpreting the sounds of Little Richard, Elvis Presley, Buddy Holly, Jerry Lee Lewis, Chuck Berry, and Fats Domino. Then they evolved as musicians, being the first to blend the sounds of a classical orchestra with those of a rock group, the first to use feedback, and among the first—with the help of producer George Martin—to use the technology of a recording studio in many new and exciting ways (running tapes backwards, using distortion, and re-editing tapes, for example). The Beatles were also the first to print lyrics and liner notes on their album covers, the first to create an album that tied songs together thematically, and among the first to write popular songs about drugs and psychedelic experiences.

The effect of the Beatles on popular music is so great that it almost cannot be fully assessed. However, one measure of their influence is their acknowledged and obvious impact on the music of many of the top-rated recording artists, even of the 1990s. Billy Joel, Prince, Sting, Elton John, Phil Collins, Spin Doctors, Counting Crows, and dozens of others owe the evolution of their sound in some way to the Beatles.

Today, music critics and analysts are still discussing the impact of the Beatles—not only on music but also on popular culture. This band, probably more than any other, embodied the spirit of the sixties and helped to create it. Their music gave voice to a generation of young people who were eager to question and redefine everything about their society. Fashion, visual arts, and popular music were just a few of the areas that underwent complete re-evaluation and redesign during this period. What is most impressive about the music of the Beatles—mostly that of Lennon and McCartney—is how well it has transcended the era from which it sprang. Amazingly, Beatles music is still not only popular in the 1990s, but much of it seems just as relevant and contemporary in feeling as any music being written today.

This is the story of the creative partnership that drove the Beatles. It is a story of emotional and artistic complexity; of mutual love and mutual hate; of seemingly polar opposites who came together through a series of mostly random coincidences. When the special ingredients of the Lennon-McCartney partnership were mixed together, they formed the core of what is indisputably the single most popular and influential band in the history of popular music.

Chapter

John Lennon, Rebel

"All the boys my age are getting guitars,

can you lend me the money to get one?"

—*Young John to his Aunt Mimi*

Alfred Lennon, John's father, was an absentee parent from the time of his son's birth. Working as a steward on various cruise ships, "Freddy" spent his days aboard one ocean liner or another, headed for far-off places like New York and South America. Freddy was the son of an Irish freight clerk named John whose original surname—from Galway, Ireland—was O'Leannain.

John O'Leannain, John's grandfather, was born in 1912, in England, one of six children. He had been, at one point, an occasional singer who spent part of his life in a musical group in America. The elder O'Leannain died of a diseased liver when Freddy was only nine years old. The loss of his father at a young age may explain why Freddy seemed unable to act as much of a parent to John throughout his life.

John Lennon's mother was born Julia Stanley in Liverpool, England, in 1914, the youngest of five daughters. Julia's father was a salvage official with the Liverpool Salvage Company who spent his days retrieving submarines from the bottom of the Atlantic Ocean. His father, John's great grandfather, had a career as a professional musician. Julia grew up in Liverpool and worked as an usherette in a local movie theater before she met, and fell in love with, Alfred Lennon. They were married on December 3, 1938.

On October 9, 1940, Julia gave birth to a son—named John Winston Lennon—at Oxford Street Maternity Hospital in Liverpool. His middle name was an effort to honor Britain's Prime Minister at the time, Winston Churchill, who was bravely guiding England through a frightening and devastating war with Adolf Hitler and the Axis powers. In fact, on the night John was born, Hitler's air force—called the *Luftwaffe*—pounded Liverpool with one of the fiercest bombings of World War II. Liverpool was not only one of England's largest cities, it was also a major port. For this reason, it was a strategic target and was vulnerable to constant attack. Only a few hours old, John was placed under a hospital bed for safety during the dangerous bombing raids that plagued the city. A week later, infant and mother were sent home to 9 Newcastle Road, in Wavetree, a suburb of Liverpool.

As John's first three or four years went by, Julia became more and more unhappy with the pressures and limitations of acting as a single parent. The increasing strain caused by Freddy's constant absence and lack of communication created an insurmountable obstacle for their marriage. Julia finally decided to divorce Freddy and seek companionship elsewhere.

In 1944, Julia met an army officer while she was a waitress at a diner in Penny Lane, on the outskirts of Liverpool. After only a short while, she became pregnant, and the father disappeared, never to be seen again. The resulting baby, John's half-sister, was born in June 1945, and was named Victoria Elizabeth. Unable to cope with caring for two children alone, Julia surrendered the infant for adoption to a family in Norway, and no one in the Lennon family has ever contacted her since. It is most likely that, to this day, the woman who was born Victoria Elizabeth does not know that she is the half-sister of one of the world's most famous and influential people.

Julia eventually established a more stable relationship with a hotel waiter named John Dykins. In 1945, he moved in with her in Liverpool and became stepdad to five-year-old John. Though Julia and Dykins were perfectly contented with their new family arrangement, Julia's sister Mimi did not think there was enough stability for her young nephew. Mimi insisted that John should be provided with a better environment. The local social work agency agreed, and John was moved into the comfortable and ever-so-stable middle-class home of his Aunt Mimi and Uncle George in the suburb of Woolton, at 251 Menlove Avenue.

Life for John in Woolton was, on the surface, quite enviable. Mimi doted on and pampered her young nephew, always putting his interests before everything else. George, who ran a dairy farm, often took his young nephew out to see the cows being milked or fed. George was the first real fatherly influence John had ever known, and their time together was precious to the young boy. George had taught John to read and write at age four. It was also at this age that John received his first cheap guitar, a gift from Julia. Although he did not play it all the time, the instrument became one of his earliest and most coveted personal possessions.

During this time, just as John was settling into a comfortable and predictable life, his father Freddy reappeared in an effort to reclaim his rights to his son. Caught in the middle of all the bitterness between his parents, John was forced to choose sides between his father, his mother, and his aunt and uncle. For the five-year-old child, the sudden return of his father precipitated one of the most traumatic periods of John Lennon's childhood.

John's headmaster in primary school described him as "sharp as a needle."

The effects of this domestic trauma would soon show themselves in other areas of John's life. At Dovedale Primary School, near Penny Lane, John—age five—had already become something of a discipline problem. The school's headmaster described him as "sharp as a needle, but he won't do anything he doesn't want to do." The profile of the iconoclast and rebel was already taking shape. As he learned to hide his emotions, John channeled his anger toward authority figures and lashed out against those who tried to control him.

After being with John Dykins for about a year, Julia became pregnant once again. In 1947, she gave birth to a baby girl, whom she and Dykins named Julia. In 1949, another daughter was born, named Jacqui Gertrude. Both girls took the last name of Dykins, even though their parents were never married.

As young John went through primary school, books and reading—rather than toys—became his passion. One of his favorite stories was *Alice in Wonderland* by Lewis Carroll. Fascinated by the sound of words and the use of language, the boy memorized passages of the fairy tale and recited them often. Later, as an adult, John would fall in love with another famous Lewis Carroll work, *Jabberwock*, which used language in a comedic, playful, and fantastic way. The young lad also developed a passion for painting and drawing in bed, and art became John's major interest in primary school. By age ten, he had also received a harmonica from his Uncle George, which prompted a new interest in music.

In 1952, John graduated from Dovedale and entered Quarry Bank High School in Woolton. By this time, his fondness for insults and getting into trouble had become finely developed. He cared little for schoolwork and preferred to spend most of his days causing trouble. This did not mean, however, that John Lennon was lazy. In fact, he put a great deal of creative energy into being such a problem. Most of his talent was spent in mocking his teachers, doing obscene drawings, and writing cruel and insulting poems about people he disliked.

His classmates, and even many of his teachers, recognized the great talent in the young Lennon, however misdirected it may have been. Many even admired his resourcefulness and cleverness. When he recalled those early days, John said, "I had a feeling I was either a genius or a madman. Now I know I wasn't a madman, so I must have been a genius." Of course, not everyone agreed with John's assessment. Quarry Bank's headmaster remembered the young boy as someone who was "an under-achiever, who made no really positive contribution to the life of the school."

Even if John was a genius, he was a genius who spent more time in school being disciplined than learning. Although many recognized his raw potential, his antics continually threatened the orderly running of the institution. Consequently, John was on the verge of expulsion numerous times.

The loss of his Uncle George in 1954, when John was just fourteen, was a great blow. Because Freddy had vanished again after his last appearance, losing George was like losing a father for the second time. For the rest of his life, John would continue to search for another father figure who would take him under his wing and show him the strict but caring discipline of love.

"I had a feeling I was either a genius or a madman."

The anger, confusion, and heartbreak John felt after his uncle's death only seemed to fuel his rebellious nature. John and his angel-faced sidekick, Pete Shotten, elevated disrespect and rule-breaking to an art. Together, they skipped classes, smoked cigarettes, cursed and yelled in the hallways, and stole from classmates and teachers. Both boys dressed like slobs, had serious attitude problems, and did not at all care what anyone thought about them. Though most people who knew John recognized his potential for genius, many were nonetheless convinced his behavior would eventually land him on a breadline or in jail.

During this time of declining schoolwork and general defiance, John began to visit his mother more often. In some ways, the young man must have taken comfort in being with his mother, not only for the solace of family but also because he identified many of his own rebellious traits in her. Julia had always been somewhat irreverent in her life. She was known to question authority and to live life on her own terms. Her independent streak was evidenced particularly by her choice of family life; having two babies without marrying Dykins raised many eyebrows in the 1940s, particularly her sister Mimi's.

It was while spending time with Julia that John was also able to further explore his interest in music. Julia, who could play the banjo in a limited way, made an effort to teach John a few chords. Once they established their repertoire together, John and his mother would sing and play together for hours on end.

As John grew into his early teens and became more interested in music, he began to search for a personal identity. Around the time he turned fifteen, three ground-breaking movies from America appeared in the Liverpool cinemas. The first was *Rebel Without a Cause*, starring Hollywood's newest brooding heartthrob, James Dean. In this movie about the utter restlessness and confusion of youth, Dean and the other teenage characters react with anger and self-destructiveness to the senseless world their parents have made. The second film was *Blackboard Jungle*, a story of schoolboy aggression that reflected a sharp, bleak view of modern life. *Rock Around the Clock*, starring the music sensation Bill Haley and The Comets, lacked any coherent message or story line but was an entertaining vehicle for proving that a new rock 'n' roll lifestyle had definitely arrived.

The young characters in these three movies seemed to be speaking directly to John Lennon. In them, he found an attitude, an image, and a style of music that spoke to—even celebrated— the anger and rebelliousness he felt. From that point on, John considered himself a rock 'n' roller, pure and simple.

It was also during the mid-1950s that a British musician by the name of Lonnie

Donegan formalized the "skiffle craze" in England. Skiffle was a low-tech musical style in which groups of kids got together and "jammed" on beat-up old instruments and washboards in small bars and halls. Because the emphasis was on the act of making music rather than on expensive instruments or great musicianship, thousands of young teens throughout England eagerly joined together and formed loosely organized but energetic skiffle bands.

It was primarily the emergence of skiffle music that prompted John to organize his own band. First, he went to his Aunt Mimi and said, "All the boys my age are getting guitars, can you lend me the money to get one?" Mimi, however, did not agree. Next, John went to his mother, but she also was unable to help. Finally, he ordered a guitar from a catalog at a cost of £5, or about $9. Once the guitar arrived, John set about rounding up some Quarry Bank friends to get his group started. He signed up classmate Rod Davis on banjo and another friend, Eric Griffiths, on guitar. John's partner in mischief, Pete Shotten, agreed that he would learn how to play washboard.

After a few weeks of practice, John's skiffle group was already playing passable versions of a few popular standards. As the undisputed leader of the group, John was free to make any and all decisions that affected them. At this point, he decided to add another of his school chums, Colin

Hanton, on drums. The first official name of the group was the "Blackjacks." Each member wore black jeans and a plain white shirt. When John added an old Dovedale friend, Ivan Vaughan, on bass, he formally changed the name of the group to the "Quarry Men." The group was soon able to line up some formal engagements at local churches and youth clubs. After playing the first few times as a professional, John realized that he truly enjoyed the life of a musician. Aside from being able to drink and smoke freely, he was able to play music while earning enough money to keep himself happy at the local pubs.

As the Quarry Men improved their sound through practice and live performances, another major musical influence gave them inspiration. A young, irreverent boy from Tupelo, Mississippi, named Elvis Presley was becoming a worldwide phenomenon. Elvis was like nothing the world of music had ever seen. Here was a white man who not only brought the sound of black music to rock 'n' roll, but was also loud and full of raw energy and sexuality. In fact, he gyrated his hips with such force that he was officially declared by certain groups to be "obscene." (When Elvis appeared on television in the 1950s, the censors only allowed the camera to show him from the waist up!) To John Lennon, Elvis Presley was the coolest thing going. John acknowledged this influence, once saying that, after Elvis, "nothing was the same" for him.

By 1956, it was all starting to come together for John. The strident, raw energy of rock 'n' roll gave a powerful voice to restless youths around the world. As a renegade form of music, it was also an ideal teen diversion—for John it was the perfect outlet for years of pent up anger and resentment. Rock's growing power was now starting to be recognized by the so-called "establishment." Teen idols like Elvis Presley, Buddy Holly, and Bill Haley were seen as threatening and disgusting by adults the world over. For John Lennon and others like him, the fact that their parents hated rock 'n' roll was exactly what made it so great.

Chapter 2

Paul McCartney, Perfectionist

"Lose a mother and find a guitar."

—*Mike McCartney,*
on his brother's early love of music

James McCartney, Paul's father, was born on July 7, 1902, one of nine children. His father, Joseph McCartney, was a tobacco cutter who married a woman named Florence Clegg. Not particularly well-to-do, they lived in one of Liverpool's roughest neighborhoods. As a young boy, Jim was seriously interested in music and taught himself to play the piano. Into adulthood, music would continue to be a part of Jim McCartney's life—one that would greatly inspire and influence his sons, Paul and Mike. Speaking of his father today, Paul readily admits that his dad "was definitely my strongest musical influence."

James eventually became a cotton salesman in Liverpool. During his off hours, he often performed in various jazz bands that he had organized. At one point, Jim Mac's Jazz Band was one of Liverpool's most popular attractions. A talented and successful man about town, James met a local nurse named Mary Patricia Mohin. One of four children, Mary had been a nurse since the age of fourteen. Their early dates together were punctuated by the explosions of bombs from Hitler's *Luftwaffe* that were falling in Liverpool at the time. While they huddled together under doorways and in underground bomb shelters, Jim and Mary managed to grow close rather quickly.

On April 15, 1941, in Liverpool, Jim and Mary were married in a full church wedding. Their first child, James Paul, was born on June 18, 1942, in a private ward in Walton Hospital. Two years later, their second son, Peter Michael, was born.

For the most part, Paul remembers his earliest childhood days in the Liverpool suburb of Allerton as comfortable and secure. With two parents happily married and a bright future planned, there was little to worry the growing McCartney family. As Paul grew, he developed a weight problem, and, by the age of ten, had become rather chubby. Sensitive about his weight and subjected to the usual cruelties of childhood, he was often upset by the taunts of other schoolkids, who called him "Fatty."

Paul, age six, sits in an Allerton pasture with his younger brother, Michael.

Perhaps partially due to the relatively few hardships he faced early in life, Paul was able to concentrate on doing well in school. From the time he entered primary school, he was both a disciplined and committed student. In 1953, after passing the required exams without difficulty, he was admitted to the well-respected Liverpool Institute. It was there, beginning at age eleven, that his artistic eye and ability first began to blossom. It was also there that his sense of achievement and leadership were fostered. Popular with the teachers, administration, and his schoolmates, Paul used his natural knack for diplomacy to distinguish himself among his peers. He was voted "head boy" a number of times while at the "Inny," which gave him special privileges, such as assisting teachers, doing roll call, and delivering notes.

All this responsibility and notice made young Paul eager and happy to please authority. His success in leadership roles gave him the positive reinforcement he needed to evolve a strong sense of himself. At age fourteen, however, just as this crucial evolution was taking place for him, Paul's mother Mary suddenly died. She had been admitted to the hospital for a breast cancer operation and had died unexpectedly a few days later. For Paul, the loss was both devastating and a total shock. Mary had never even mentioned to her boys that she was sick. She had wanted to protect them from any undue worry. With Mary gone, it was up to Paul's two aunts, Mill and Jin, to come and help Jim take care of his boys. Like John Lennon after the death of his beloved Uncle George, Paul sought comfort from his heartbreak in music.

"Lose a mother and find a guitar," is how Paul's brother Mike once described the circumstances surrounding Paul's discovery of music. Unlike John Lennon, who was at first most interested in adopting the image and lifestyle of a musician, Paul's curiosity was sparked by the exposure and encouragement he received from his father. Of course, he also had a genuine interest in the study of music. In fact, young Paul had already been introduced to a wide variety of musical styles, from classical to show tunes to jazz.

Paul became immersed in playing the guitar after first losing interest in the piano lessons that his parents had forced upon him. (He had also sabotaged an audition for the local church choir by deliberately cracking his voice.) Before he took up the guitar full-time, Paul taught himself a few simple standards on an old trumpet he had inherited from his father. One of his favorite trumpet songs was "When the Saints Go Marching In." It was clear that the young boy had a great natural talent for music, it was just a question of how that talent would be expressed.

When Paul finally realized the depth of his love for the guitar, his involvement became

"He was lost. He didn't have time to eat or think about anything else. He played [his guitar] on the lavatory, in the bath, everywhere."

characteristically serious and thorough. He spent long hours teaching himself new chords and learning the words to all the most popular songs. Mike McCartney has even gone as far as describing Paul's love of the guitar as an obsession: "He was lost. He didn't have time to eat or think about anything else. He played it on the lavatory, in the bath, everywhere."

It was not long before Paul convinced his younger brother to join him in a musical partnership. In fact, the first-known public musical performance by Paul McCartney was in a Yorkshire talent contest. Billed as the "McCartney Brothers," Paul and Mike performed the Everly Brothers hit "Bye Bye Love." Paul realized at that point that he loved performing. He enjoyed having the full attention of a crowd and relished the applause and approval that came with it. His brother Mike, however, did not share Paul's enthusiasm. Shivering violently from stage fright both before and during their performance, Mike rushed offstage as soon as they were done to throw up into the first container he could find.

Now completely involved in music, Paul became fascinated by what was happening in the emerging world of rock 'n' roll. He listened to, and studied, all the chart-topping hits he could find—by both American and British rockers. In addition to admiring Elvis Presley, Jerry Lee Lewis, and Eddie Cochran, Paul idolized Little Richard, Fats Domino, and Buddy Holly. He constantly strived to imitate each of these legends throughout his musical career.

As he continued to progress on guitar, Paul made friends with the son of the man who drove the schoolbus each morning. That boy's name was George Harrison. Like Paul, young George was also heavily involved in guitar. The two boys started to hang out together on a regular basis,

Paul in 1956, age fourteen.

teaching each other new chords and learning the words to many of the most popular hits being played on the radio.

Paul had also made friends with an Institute classmate named Ivan Vaughan. Interested in music, Vaughan, in turn, had a friend from Quarry Bank High School named John Lennon. Because Paul and Ivan were both keen on keeping up with the latest sounds that were sweeping Liverpool, Ivan was able to convince Paul to join him in attending an upcoming church function in Woolton. Among bake sales and crafts displays, a rough, local band called the Quarry Men was to be featured at the event. Neither Paul nor Ivan had any idea just how important seeing that band at that church function would eventually be for both of them.

Chapter 3

Meeting Up

"You've got to meet John Lennon,

you'll get on well with him."

—*Mutual friend Ivan Vaughan to Paul*

By the time John was seventeen, the skiffle craze and Quarry Men were both in full swing. When St. Peter's, the local church in John's neighborhood, offered his band an opportunity to perform, John accepted—although reluctantly. The event was to be a kind of "garden party," with tea drinking, homemade cakes on sale, and children playing games on the lawn. It was not exactly what the rebel John thought of as a "perfect gig." The Quarry Men, however, had been without work for a while and were looking for any opportunity they could find.

It was a bright, sunny day on July 6, 1957, when the rough-and-ready band arrived to set up in a field near the church. As they worked their way through their first set, John noticed an unexpected but familiar face walking through the crowd. It was his Aunt Mimi. Almost immediately, the young leather-clad tough stood up straighter and tried to appear less drunk. Mimi, who had no idea it was John's band that would be playing, stood facing the stage, transfixed. This was the first time she had ever seen her John perform, and, as she watched, she became noticeably overcome with pride.

Another person standing in the crowd was sixteen-year-old Paul McCartney. Paul was only attending the show at the insistence of Ivan

Vaughan, who knew Paul as a talented young musician who was serious about rock 'n' roll. It was Ivan who first suggested to Paul, "You've got to meet John Lennon, you'll get on well with him."

Ivan and Paul stood in the crowd, listening as the Quarry Men pounded through their set. Even though Paul thought their music was primitive, he was duly impressed by the fact that a bunch of scruffy seventeen-year-olds had organized their own group and were actually playing. John, being the obvious leader of the band, impressed Paul the most.

After the show, Ivan brought Paul over to John. In an interview many years later, Paul remembered his first encounter with John: "I was a fat schoolboy and, as he leaned an arm on my shoulder, I realized he was drunk." After talking a bit about music and skiffle, John was impressed to learn that Paul not only knew the chords for many cool songs, but that he also could write down the full lyrics to the Eddie Cochran smash "Twenty Flight Rock" and Gene Vincent's bubbly blues hit "Be-Bop-A-Lula." The head Quarry Man was doubly impressed that young Paul could actually tune a guitar on his own. Because this was something none of the Quarry Men could do, John saw that Paul's talent might be useful to the band. If nothing else, John reasoned, Paul's tuning ability could hold a certain promise for their sound.

As John became more serious about pursuing a life in music, he also began to mature personally. After his chance meeting with Paul, John realized—perhaps for the first time in his life—that other people might have talents to add to the group that were equal to his. That night, after meeting Paul, John wrestled with a big question. Should he let the boy from Allerton into his group? As John contemplated the question, he also realized that he was reluctant to concede any control to someone else. On the other hand, he thought, Paul was a stronger guitarist, had a better knowledge of rock 'n' roll songs, and could provide great strength musically to the group. Looking back years later, John remembered his thoughts as he went through the decision process:

> I had a group. I was the singer, and the leader. I met Paul and made a decision whether or not to have him in the group. Was it better to have a guy who was better than the people I already had in, or not? To make the band stronger or make me be stronger?

Although John felt threatened, he realized that if he was serious about making music his life, he needed to invite Paul to join. It was one of the first truly responsible decisions the young, undisciplined teenager had ever made. It was John's friend Pete Shotten who passed the news of the decision to Paul a few days later. "John wants you in the group," Pete exclaimed, as if

Paul had won the lottery. Even though Paul was secretly elated, he decided to play it cool. He offhandedly said that it would be at least two months before he could actually join—he had made plans to attend a nearby scout camp for the summer first.

When the summer of 1957 came to an end, John entered the Liverpool College of Art. Addicted to fried foods—classmates swore he ate nothing but fish and chips—John constantly reeked of oil and cigarette smoke. He also fostered his tough "teddy boy" look—the U.K. version of a James Dean or Elvis Presley style—characterized by a long, greased-back D.A. haircut, sideburns, and tight trousers. At a time when most of his schoolmates were still wearing crew cuts and neatly styled clothes, this gave John the air of nonconformity he craved. For him, nothing was more important than individuality. And now that he was in art college, John decided to cultivate his rebel image even more. He enlisted his "hip" classmate, Stuart Sutcliffe, to help him in this regard. Reveling in the "art student" bohemian lifestyle, John and Stuart became the best of friends.

Being a Quarry Man now, Paul began to spend a great deal of time hanging out with John. Getting together regularly was easy. The Liverpool Institute—which Paul, his brother Mike, George Harrison, and Ivan Vaughan attended—was right around the corner from the art college. John, Paul, Ivan, and fellow Quarry Man, Len Garry, would hold regular lunchtime jam sessions in Professor Ballard's classroom at the art college. Each day, they played for an hour or two, running through their standard list of Buddy Holly and Everly Brothers favorites.

Paul's first steady gig with the Quarry Men started on October 18, 1957, at a Liverpool music club. Their list of songs, like those of most other local skiffle groups, consisted only of "covers"—imitative versions of already established popular hits. Playing the same old list night after night, both John and Paul became increasingly bored. It was this boredom that prompted Paul to write the first original composition ever performed by the Quarry Men. Paul's song, entitled "I Lost My Little Girl," greatly impressed John. It also sparked John's highly competitive nature and inspired him to start writing songs as well. One of John's earliest tunes from this period was a personal ditty entitled "Winston's Walk."

A few months after they met, John and Paul began playing secretly at Paul's house while Paul's dad was out. There, the pair wrote songs as a team for the first time. The creative elements that each writer brought to the mix then would endure throughout their musical lives together. John was the cynical, hard-edged poet who enjoyed creating cryptic messages and playing with words. Paul was the romantic with an optimistic view of the world who always made an effort not to insult or upset anyone. Due to his more thorough knowledge of music, Paul often concentrated more attention on his melodies than his words. By contrast, John tended to be more intrigued by the overall message of his music than the notes that made it up. Though Paul was by far the more accomplished musician, John offered him a raw, emotional, and rebellious quality that he lacked—it was the very essence of rock 'n' roll. Soon after they began writing together, John and Paul realized that they needed each other in a profound way. Neither believed he could make it in the music world without the artistic balance offered by the other.

In a biography, Paul recalled his early working relationship with John: "Gradually we started to write stuff together. Which didn't mean we wrote *everything* together...." During their first three years together, however, John and Paul wrote dozens of songs as a team. Many of these early collaborations were copied down in a spiral notebook that, unfortunately, was lost. Some of the tunes, however, have survived. Songs such as "Catswalk," "Hot as Sun," "Just Fun," "Keep Looking That Way," and "Thinking of Linking," remain in existence but have never officially been released on any album. Other early compositions, such as "When I'm Sixty-Four" (written by Paul at age sixteen),

"Love Me Do," "I Saw Her Standing There," and "One After 909" were released with great success on various Beatles albums during the years that followed.

Because of Paul's broader knowledge of music, he was much more serious about the instruments he played and wanted to study and learn as much as he could about each one. Paul's tastes ran not only to rock 'n' roll but also to classical, jazz, and show music. John, who was initially drawn to the "music scene" primarily to color his image as an "artist," realized only later that music was also an important emotional outlet for him. It was John's ability to bring the philosophy of rock 'n' roll into the band that made all the rest possible. Although the two had somewhat different approaches to music, these differences only brought strength to their song-writing collaboration.

Most of the joy John and Paul first shared was in the music they played together. But, as the two worked together more and more, it became obvious that there was another element emerging. It seemed that, the more John wrote, the more Paul was inspired. And the better Paul's songs got, the more John was driven to improve his writing. For Paul, having a partner with a drive and enthusiasm for music equal to his own was just what he needed. Paul respected John not so much for his playing, but for his self-motivation, his ability to organize a group, and even for his determination to start writing songs of his own.

The major dynamic of this early partnership was now becoming clear. It was, more than anything, creativity based on competition. Neither writer wanted to be outdone by the other. As soon as Paul finished a song and played it for John, for example, hearing it would prompt John to write a tune that captured the qualities he admired in Paul's writing. If Paul was stuck without a middle or a bridge for a song, John would often step in and suggest a great solution. The give-and-take that developed between them as artists would continue to strengthen in the coming months. It was this uniquely powerful "creative rivalry" that kept the Lennon & McCartney team together, fueling their incredible productivity for many years.

A Taste of Success

"The difference between us is that

John doesn't care what people

think of him. I do."

—Paul McCartney

As John and Paul continued through their respective school programs in 1958, the rest of the world was changing rapidly. Post-war Britain had by now evolved from mourning and uncertainty to prosperity. At the same time, the outspoken, feisty Communist, Nikita Khrushchev, had become premier of the USSR. Khrushchev's fervent anti-democracy policies effectively began an era known as the Cold War, when the proliferation of nuclear arms and other threats made Soviet relations with many Western powers particularly tense. The onset of the Cold War ironically coincided with the first successful transatlantic jet service, which connected the United States to the countries across the Atlantic in Europe, including Britain. In Liverpool, John Lennon's radio was permanently tuned to Radio Luxembourg, which played every American smash hit, from Elvis's "Jailhouse Rock" to Jerry Lee Lewis's "Great Balls of Fire" to Buddy Holly's "It Doesn't Matter Anymore."

In July, tragedy once again touched the personal life of John Lennon. Julia was struck and killed by a hit-and-run driver as she left her sister Mimi's house in Woolton. John, now age eighteen, was devastated by the loss. Despite his suffering, he never outwardly showed his emotion or spoke to anyone about his mother's death. Although he felt the pain deeply, he had, by now, become an expert at burying his despair. It was during this time that he began to drink more heavily, taking refuge in the noise and distractions of the local pubs.

Paul McCartney was, in fact, the only person who could really understand the pain his partner was going through. Having lost his mother only two years earlier, Paul tried his best to reach out to John at a critical time, helping him funnel his anger and despair into the creative endeavors of music. Paul's compassion and levelheadedness proved to be a crucial anchor for John during this terrible period. Their shared life experiences—though both tragic—created a powerful additional bond between the two young men.

Without the structure, discipline, and direction that Paul brought to their partnership, John might have allowed his anger over Julia's death to destroy whatever creativity and discipline he had. Michael Isaacson, one of John's Quarry Bank classmates, recalled John's volatile nature: "If he hadn't become famous, his anger could have been vented in another direction. Where his energy was channeled into creative music, it would have gone into something destructive instead of creative. He was strictly an all-or-nothing kind of guy." Many observers believe that, without Paul's support, the musical career of John Lennon could have conceivably ended in 1958.

It was Paul who suggested that they consider letting his old friend, George Harrison, into the Quarry Men. Young George was eager, he hero-worshiped John. Paul remembers that his partner's initial reaction to the idea of asking a boy three years younger than they to join the group was "no way!" After further convincing by Paul, however, John agreed to hear the "little kid" audition. George's natural talent and ability to play in different styles finally sold the Quarry Men's leader on him. The fact that George's mother was also happy to allow the band to rehearse in her house probably weighed in George's favor as well.

With a new guitarist on board, the Quarry Men continued to perform at local pubs and music clubs. Bored with the "dated" image their name projected, John decided to change the band's title to "Johnny and the Moondogs" in 1959. That same year, another person's death brought great despair to John, as well as to many others. While flying to a performance, Buddy Holly's plane crashed, killing him along with two rising rock stars, Richie Valens and the "Big Bopper." Buddy Holly had been an enormous influence on John, who felt that the American star embodied the very spirit of rock 'n' roll. John reacted to Holly's death as if it were a death in his own family. Again, for a while, John mourned privately and seemed to detach himself from the world around him.

Still cultivating his "artist" image, John plodded somewhat aimlessly through his courses at the art college. Except for the few times he allowed his best friend, art classmate Stuart Sutcliffe, to convince him to pursue painting more seriously, John continued to develop his musical interests at the expense of his formal studies. It was also in art college that John met fellow student Cynthia Powell. A "proper" girl who liked John's outrageous nature, Cynthia would soon become John's first long, serious relationship. (She would also eventually become his wife.) Cynthia remembered years later that, when she and John first became serious in 1959, John was consumed with his music. He was also, by her account, excited and genuinely inspired by the partnership that was developing between him and Paul.

In fact, 1959 was a significant year in the history of the Lennon & McCartney team. It was then that John and Paul formally shook hands on an agreement they had previously made with each other. They agreed that, from that time on—whether a song was written by either of them individually or both together— the credit would read "Lennon-McCartney." Although it was a naive and idealistic way to do things from a business standpoint, this special arrangement marked an honest and tender show of mutual respect and affection between the two.

By now, it was more than just musical convenience that kept John and Paul together. Theirs was a true relationship. Creatively, they were feeding off each other in constantly new and exciting ways. In fact, by mid-1959, they were spending as much time together, playing and writing songs, as they possibly could. As their partnership flourished, they would skip more and more full days of school so that they could devote more time to practice and new music. And as they progressed, each partner continued to feel he needed the spark of the other to help define his material. Paul's influence tempered John's angry and aggressive side and brought out the tender romance bubbling not too far below the surface. John, in turn, gave a much-needed "bite" to Paul's work, which, at times, suffered from overbearing sweetness. John was often the one to add a clever or poetic phrase to a Paul lyric stuck in simple realism.

By the end of 1959, John and Paul were becoming more ambitious and determined to achieve greater success in music. With this in mind, John decided that their name—which had bounced back and forth between the Quarry Men and Johnny and the Moondogs—sounded too boring. A new name would not only help them redefine their direction, it would also give them broader appeal.

For John and Paul, no one in the pop scene could compare with the late, great Buddy Holly.

Both writers emulated him in their compositions as well as with their vocal stylings and rhythms. John had always admired the name of Holly's back-up group, "the Crickets," and he and Paul played around with various names that would pay homage to their idol. It was Quarry Man pal Stuart Sutcliffe, however, who first uttered the name "Beetles" as a play on the Crickets. The other boys loved the idea, but were not convinced of the name. John, at the same time, wanted to come up with something that would incorporate the hippest new buzz word in music at the time: "beat." With this in mind, the band was first renamed "The Silver Beats," then officially changed to the "Silver Beetles" for a while in 1959. Finally, John—the ultimate word punster—decided to blend the two concepts by spelling the band's name "Beatals." From there, it was only a short leap to the final spelling, "Beatles." In June 1960, the group performed its first official engagement ever as the Beatles.

Thanks to a local Liverpool entrepreneur named Allan Williams, more gigs were soon to follow for the Beatles, who had by now acquired a young local named Pete Best as their regular drummer. Williams first secured bookings for the group around England. As they gained a more impressive following, he decided to market the Beatles abroad—specifically to Hamburg, Germany, where British pop groups had recently come much into fashion. Hamburg, however,

It was Stuart Sutcliffe who first uttered the name "Beetles."

was a rough place filled with illicit sex, drunks, drugs, and street toughs from all over. It took some convincing to get the boys' parents to agree to even let them go to the infamous city of Hamburg. Regaled with promises and assurances from both Williams and the bandmembers, the parents were finally convinced that this was the big break their sons had been waiting for.

On August 16, 1960, the Beatles set sail for Hamburg. What they found when they arrived exceeded even the scariest rumors they had heard. Prostitutes and drug addicts were everywhere. Violence and vandalism were rampant. But, for these young Liverpool boys (John was still only nineteen, Paul eighteen, and George, not even seventeen), it was their first chance to enjoy true independence and to experience the most exciting city they had ever seen.

Whatever Allan Williams promised the parents back home, it was abandoned as soon as the group set foot in Hamburg. Put up in disgusting hotel rooms and required to play grueling schedules, the boys in the band were forced to seriously adjust their expectations of fame and fortune. While booked at the Indra Club, they played from 8:00 p.m. to 2:00 a.m., banging out six sets a night of forty-five minutes each. Playing for so many hours straight on a constant basis was exhausting, but it forced John and Paul to increase the band's repertoire and to hone their survival skills on stage. In an interview in

This rare photo, taken by John Lennon, shows the band and its friends on their way to Hamburg in 1960. Standing, left, is Allan Williams; standing, right, is Stuart Sutcliffe. Paul sits center, with George Harrison and drummer Pete Best seated right.

1971, John recalled the scene in Hamburg: "Virtually every night at the Indra some poor bastard was either bottled or knifed, or worse. Fortunately…we were generally left alone."

Not all of their Hamburg experience was so depressing. During their first stay, the band gained a special fan named Astrid Kirchherr. Astrid had first been brought to hear the Beatles by her artist boyfriend, Klaus Voorman. Astrid's effect on the group would turn out to be quite significant. Aside from offering them some genuine comfort and protection in a dangerous and cold city, she taught them all a great deal about style. Astrid, an avant-garde "bohemian," managed to influence their choice of dress, their personal lifestyles, and even their music. She had adopted the classic "all-black look" and successfully convinced the boys of its hipness. From that time on, the Beatles shed their conventional "teddy boy" looks for a decidedly more bohemian image.

Before the band's contract at the Indra was up, some locals prompted authorities to deport George, who they said was too young to be working. Then Paul and Pete were ordered to leave for allegedly setting fire to their hotel room (a trumped-up charge they deny to this day). Unable to continue performing alone, John left Hamburg as well. The boys arrived in the port of Liverpool weary, dejected, and penniless. Unconvinced that careers in music would ever be possible, each bandmember crawled home to think things over and make their excuses to waiting parents.

Fed up with empty promises, Paul's father forced his son to get a "respectable job." Paul became a delivery boy for a Liverpool company called Speedy Prompt Delivery Service. This position, however, was over in only a few weeks. From there, Paul got a job as a lowly coil winder in a copper wire factory. Each day, he spent his eight hours at work rolling miles of copper wire onto a giant spool.

Paul, like John, could not tolerate the drudgery of regular work—certainly not after getting a taste of the exciting and unpredictable life of a performer and professional musician. It is partly for this reason that their first trip to Hamburg would ultimately turn out to be the most important trip in the history of the group. Although it was disappointing and exhausting, it challenged and hardened them in many vital ways. The unfriendly audiences, the grueling performance schedules, and the terrible living conditions gave them a dose of reality about life on the road. All these elements also forced the group to tighten itself musically and to become much more confident performers on stage. As it turned out, if it had not been for the rigors of Hamburg, the Beatles would not have been as prepared for the pressures they were about to face as the world's most popular band.

Chapter **5**

Breakthroughs

John: Where are we going fellas?

Paul, George, Ringo: To the top,

Johnny, to the top!

John: And where is the top, fellas?

Paul, George, Ringo: To the toppermost

of the poppermost!

—*Traditional Beatle morale-booster*

Though they could not have expected it when they returned from their first Hamburg trip, the events of 1961 would soon sweep the band up into a dizzying whirlwind of pressure and fame.

The Beatles at this point were without Stuart Sutcliffe. He had stayed behind in Hamburg to be with his newfound love, Astrid. With Pete Best still on drums, however, they began to play more regularly at a club owned by Mona Best, Pete's mom. The Casbah Club was similar to the Indra in Hamburg—dark, loud, and smoky—but it was considerably safer.

By now, the group was starting to develop a real following. Their stint in Germany added greatly to their mystique as well as to their music, and their look and sound were finally being noticed. Their popularity by March 1961 was sufficient for them to be booked at the trendy Cavern Club. There, they drew solid audiences and gained valuable exposure in Liverpool's music circuit. Within weeks, the Beatles had become so popular that they were booked for Monday, Wednesday, and Friday lunches and Wednesday and Sunday nights on a regular basis. Paul, who had now assumed the role of bass player in the group, could boast to his father that he was bringing home more than twice what he made at his old job coiling wire.

As the group became more professional and successful, the stresses and strains of keeping the band running smoothly became greater. New conflicts between John and Paul developed during this time as well. Squabbles over which songs should be played and in which order became more frequent. Also, as Paul asserted himself more as an equal leader in the group, John became increasingly guarded. Between the two, there was a constant battle for position in the band. John always considered himself the founder and the leader of the group and was not open to giving up any control. One observer noted how the lines of power were evidenced on stage at the Cavern. "John fed off Paul, but it was John who made most of the announcements. Paul would add to what John said, but John made most of the first moves."

Their behavior on stage was not always completely true to their personalities. Each member was by now acutely aware of the role he played as a defined "character" in the group. Different fans were attracted to different members for different reasons. Some were attracted to John's tough, abrasive, masculinity. Others were melted by Paul's romantic disposition and gooey, boyish charm. Still others simply swooned at Pete Best's reticence and rough good looks.

The fact that each member of the band attracted his own following was a relatively new phenomenon at the time. It was also most likely

The Beatles, live on stage at the Cavern in Liverpool, 1961.

a key to their great success. Whereas other groups had a definite "front man" and a bunch of relatively nameless backup musicians, John and Paul shared the spotlight, with George occasionally taking center stage. Paul was warm and friendly with the fans. John kept his distance and was moody. They were perfect foils for each other. Whenever John offended the audience or became abrasive, Paul would be there to apologize and smooth things out. At the same time, without John's rebellious edge, the group might not have been perceived as very "hip" or "rock 'n' roll," and, as a result, the fans might have lost interest.

In March 1961, the Beatles were ready to make their second trip to Hamburg. Although this trip entailed the same grueling working conditions and the same abysmal living conditions as the first, at least the money was better this time. The one significant benefit of this trip was that it provided them the opportunity to have their first professional recording session with the popular British rocker, Tony Sheridan. Of the songs recorded during that session, a rocking version of "My Bonnie" was released as a single. In only a short time, it reached number five on the West German hit parade and went on to sell more than 100,000 copies. Because the Beatles had done the session for a one-time fee, they had surrendered all future rights to royalties in the recordings. To add to that bum deal, they were not even properly credited on the Sheridan album, which billed them as "The Beat Brothers."

The limited success of "My Bonnie," even though the group did not reap any financial rewards, was encouraging and important. It not only gave the Beatles a small taste of worldwide popularity, it also caused them to focus more on thinking about the need for business management. In the future, they decided, they must avoid letting others take advantage of them financially.

By the fall of 1961, their steady appearances in Liverpool and their exposure abroad caused the Beatles' popularity to spread like wildfire. Female fans, each of whom had chosen her favorite Beatle, would come to the Cavern at lunchtime to scream as their heartthrob sang and bobbed about.

This increasing popularity finally got the attention of local businesspeople and entrepreneurs. One of them was Brian Epstein, the twenty-seven-year-old manager of the record section in a local department store. Epstein had become interested in the group after a customer asked for them by name: On October 28, 1961, a young rock 'n' roll fan named Raymond Jones had walked into Epstein's record department and requested a copy of "My Bonnie" by the Beatles.

Epstein, who was almost exclusively a classical music lover, had never heard of the band. This, however, did not stop him. An avowed perfectionist, Epstein prided himself on being able to supply his customers with almost anything that existed in record form. If he did not have it in stock, he promised everyone, he would find it and order it. And that is just what he set out to do for Mr. Jones.

A few telephone calls turned up some helpful information for Epstein. He learned that copies of the Sheridan record were available on the Polydor label, and he ordered a few hundred right away. Soon after that, Epstein realized by a fluke that this group with the funny name was actually playing just a few hundred yards down the street at the Cavern. Curious, he decided to check them out in person.

"I had never seen anything like the Beatles on any stage," Brian Epstein said.

Epstein went to the Cavern one November night in 1961 and was instantly attracted to the four boys he saw performing. "I had never seen anything like the Beatles on any stage," Epstein later wrote in his book, *A Cellarful of Noise.* "They smoked as they played, and they ate and talked and pretended to hit each other. They turned their backs on the audience and shouted at them and laughed at private jokes." Epstein was completely fascinated by the band, and, though they were quite a departure from his taste, he understood their appeal immediately.

Later, in December, Epstein invited the Beatles to his record store. As they talked, Epstein convinced them that he had important connections in the music industry and could really do something to promote them. Ready to leave the routine of the Cavern and advance their careers, they agreed to let Brian Epstein become the manager of the Beatles.

From the moment Epstein took the helm, the image of the group changed. First, he insisted that they be on time for everything: gigs, meetings, promotions. Second, they were to stop eating and drinking and chewing gum on stage, and they were not allowed to shout at the audience. He also insisted on a "tighter sound" and a song set that was a maximum of an hour. Using the success of other local groups as an example, Epstein also insisted that they wear suits, shirts, and ties as part of their look.

Personality differences between Paul and John became obvious as Epstein took more and more control. John rebelled and resisted the idea of "packaging" the group. He did not want to "clean up" the act in order to make the Beatles palatable to the maximum number of people possible. Paul, on the other hand, strongly supported Epstein's strategy and saw the marketing savvy behind it. In the end, John realized that their primary concern was to be commercially successful and make money. If they were really serious about that, Paul argued, it meant giving up some of their teenage ideals about being rough and rebellious.

Just as things were coming together for the group, crushing news was delivered. As they arrived in Hamburg for another stay on April 10, 1962, Astrid told them that Stuart Sutcliffe had died. When he heard the news, John burst into uncontrollable laughter, which was one odd way he had learned to deal with shock. Sutcliffe's death was yet another crucial loss for John, and one that affected him deeply. As he had before, John kept certain friends around him who would help him stay focused. Without the discipline and structure that Paul and Brian Epstein offered, John might once again have gone a very different way. In her book, *The Life of John*, Cynthia Lennon looked back to this time. She believed that without Paul to press him into writing, John's son Julian (born in 1963) to motivate him to earn some money, and Brian Epstein to manage and push him, John "would have ended up a bum."

Their third trip to Hamburg that April had begun with sadness, but it was also punctuated with some great developments. In May, the group received an urgent telegram from Epstein announcing that he had finally signed a record deal with EMI. He had already been turned down by most of the other major studios and had few options left. The fact that he was able to sign a deal with the Parlaphone division of EMI was a major achievement for the young manager.

With a recording contract signed and their popularity exploding, the Beatles were now eager to make their next move. Despite their growing success, none of them anticipated more than a moderate level of notoriety and financial security that would come from being well-liked musicians. What they did not count on was the possibility that, within weeks, they would become the most popular group in all of Britain.

Runaway Train

"I'm sorry Mr. Epstein, but groups

with guitars are definitely on the way out."

—Decca Records Recording Manager,
Dick Rowe, after hearing a few sample
Beatles tracks in 1962

By August 1962, the Beatles were ready to begin recording in an EMI studio. Poised to make the most important record of their career, they were all a bit nervous and anxious to proceed with caution. On August 16—after heated discussions among John, Paul, George, and Brian Epstein—Pete Best was suddenly fired from the group. It was a shocking blow to Best, who had been with the band since before their first trip to Hamburg and had paid his dues along with the others. Now, just on the brink of Beatles mega-success, he was being cut out. The official explanation given to him was that he was not considered a good enough drummer for the demanding standards of a recording studio. (Privately, others have speculated that it was mostly Paul's work that got Best fired. Recognized as the "best-looking" Beatle, Best supposedly posed a threat to the jealous Paul, who felt the role of heartthrob was reserved for him.) Whatever the reasons, Pete Best was summarily stripped of all his involvements in the group that August day. Two days later, on August 18, "Rory Storm and the Hurricanes" drummer Richard Starkey—known as Ringo Starr—was officially inducted as a Beatle. (Perhaps it was coincidence, but Ringo, with his large nose and curled upper lip, certainly posed little threat to Paul in the looks department.)

A formal portrait of the Beatles in 1962, shortly before Pete Best was replaced.

Ready to enter the studio now, the Beatles were introduced to their producer, George Martin. Because of his genius and the enormous influence he had in shaping the sound of the group, Martin is often referred to as the "fifth Beatle." Trained as a classical pianist and oboe player, Martin was firmly grounded in serious music. Though he was a respected musician, he was considered a bit wacky and "off the wall." In many ways, he was too dynamic and creative for the staid world of classical music. George Martin was always looking for interesting new things to do. Following old formulas and patterns held little interest for him. With the raw talent he saw in the Beatles, Martin was very excited by the opportunity he had to mold their music into something not only saleable, but also new, fresh, and interesting.

Upon hearing "Love Me Do" Aunt Mimi said, "If you think you're going to make your fortune with that, you've got another think coming."

In September 1962, the "demo" of the Beatles debut single, "Love Me Do" was recorded at 3 Abbey Road, St. John's Wood, London, under the direction of the band's new producer. The song was a classic Lennon-McCartney collaboration—the verses were mostly Paul's, with John contributing the middle. When he returned to Woolton on the evening of the demo's completion, John played "Love Me Do" for his Aunt Mimi, who was not impressed. "If you think you're going to make your fortune with that," she said disapprovingly, "you've got another think [sic] coming." When the song was released in October, Mimi's words rang true: It was popular but not a runaway chart-buster.

Things were significantly different by January, however. It was then that the mostly John composition, "Please Please Me" was released. "That's more like it," Mimi said upon hearing its demo. John responded by saying, "Mimi, that's going to be number one." By the end of the month, his prediction had come true.

With two big songs released, John and Paul were now both comfortable and capable of working together to the greatest creative advantage. John knew that Paul's best qualities were precisely those he lacked himself: Paul was determined, disciplined, and a perfectionist with details. For Paul, however, it was John's quick artistic sense and his excitement in constantly finding new challenges that kept Paul growing as a songwriter. Without John to push him in new directions, Paul was much more likely to stay with a routine, especially one that worked.

As one of the only true "insiders" of the band, Brian Epstein was a keen observer of the dynamic between John and Paul. "Paul has the glamour, John the command," Epstein said. Often, too, Epstein would be put in the middle of conflicts between Paul and John. In this way, both partners used their manager to diffuse some of their one-on-one disagreements. John, who held a lot of sway with "Eppy," would often convince the manager to take his side. Paul, who liked to control things, tended to butt heads with Eppy over the important management decisions.

At the beginning of 1963, John and Paul looked back on the previous twelve months as the most exciting and draining year of their lives. During that time, they had acquired a manager, signed a long-term contract with EMI, and lost Stuart Sutcliffe and Pete Best. As if that was not enough, John had married Cynthia, who had become pregnant, and "Please Please Me" was taking the UK music world by storm.

George Martin knew that, in order to ride the surging wave of Beatle popularity, the band had to make an album fast. Given that pressure, John and Paul quickly rose to the task, calling on all the discipline and energy they had learned from Hamburg. They began spending nearly every minute of every day writing. (After dinner with Paul's girlfriend, Jane Asher, and her parents one night, John and Paul slipped off into the music room and wrote "She Loves You.")

By February, after only a few weeks of intense work, the partners were ready with a collection of new songs. They rushed into the studio at Abbey Road, recording their first album in an astounding eleven hours. When it was finished, John and Paul were struck by the strength and prolific nature of their partnership. Together, they had completed eight original songs for their debut album, which was a ground-breaking accomplishment in an era when most albums were mostly versions of other people's tunes. To accommodate the rapidly expanding Lennon-McCartney songbook, the pair created the Northern Songs corporation, which would publish all future Lennon-McCartney songs.

As a key player in the creative development of the songs, George Martin had the most unique and accurate perspective on the interaction between Paul and John. Martin believed that the strong competitive nature of their relationship was really what drove each of them. Each writer wanted to produce more and better songs than the other. Their "musical rivalry" gave their working relationship the essential spark of creative tension, one that made each of them constantly wonder what the other was about to do. "It was like a tug of war," Martin has said.

"In the studio, their rivalry was based purely on
friendship. They had a very close relationship
because, in many ways, they were both incred-
ibly similar."

Though the differences between the two
partners are a fascinating and integral part of any
discussion about them, John and Paul also
shared many notable similarities—an aspect of
their partnership that most observers have his-
torically ignored. In many ways, the "opposites
attracting" theory is too simplistic to accurately
portray the complex undercurrents of their
friendship and their creative interplay. Ray
Coleman, in his landmark biography, *Lennon*,
points out that both men presented one persona
to the world while being very different people
underneath. Paul, who projected the sweet and
straight-laced image, was, underneath, an in-
jured, controlling, perfectionist. John, who
projected a sarcastic and rebellious tough-guy
personality, was really a vulnerable romantic,
afraid to show his softer side.

"The truth is that deep down they were very
very similar indeed," George Martin once re-
marked. "Each had a soft underbelly, each was
very much hurt by certain things. John had a
very soft side to him. But you see, each had a
bitter turn of phrase and could be quite nasty to
the other, which each one expected at certain
times." Martin did go on to say, however, that,

"they did love each other very much throughout the time I knew them in the studio."

As their producer, arranger, advisor, musical authority, and techno-wizard, Martin also saw the Lennon-McCartney creativity in action. In his opinion, the collaborative process for many of their compositions was more one in which they used each other as a sounding board and critic rather than as a partner who helped to develop each note or lyric. "They were always songwriters who helped each other out with bits and pieces. One would have most of a song finished, play it to the other, and he would say: 'Well, why don't you do this?'"

Martin has also described their relationship in other terms. "Imagine two people pulling on a rope," he said, "smiling at each other and pulling all the time with all their might. The tension between the two of them made for the bond."

By May 1963—little more than a month after the birth of John's son, Julian—the Beatles' first LP, *Please Please Me*, topped the influential Melody Maker music charts in Britain. By September, a single from the album, "She Loves You," had rocketed to the top of the British charts, with $2.5 million in sales. As November approached, another single, "I Want to Hold Your Hand," shot to the top of the charts in Britain, just before their second LP, *With the Beatles*, was released with a record-breaking advance order of 2.5 million copies. Even the

"The tension between the two of them made for the bond."

biggest rock sensation in history to date—Elvis Presley—had never been able to do that.

The optimism and charm that the Beatles represented during this time was a welcome diversion from the social upheaval and political change that took place in 1963. That year, in the midst of the Cold War, the first direct line between the White House and the Kremlin was established. It was also in 1963 that Pope John XXIII died at the age of eighty-one, and John F. Kennedy visited the Berlin Wall to deliver his famous "Ich bin eine Berliner" speech. In Washington, D.C., the Reverend Martin Luther King

John and Paul tune up backstage before a performance in 1963.

also gave a landmark speech, entitled "I Have a Dream," which gave eloquent voice to the civil rights movement that was gaining momentum in America. On November 22, President Kennedy was assassinated as his motorcade passed through downtown Dallas, Texas.

All this social and political change, however, could not dampen the world's enthusiasm for the four "moptops" from Liverpool. Their boyish playfulness and their infectious melodies made them an almost irresistible package. And their musical abilities did not go unrecognized, either. By the end of 1963, none other than the upstanding London *Times* heralded Lennon and McCartney as the "outstanding English composers of 1963." Not a bad achievement for two young Liverpool lads, ages twenty-three and twenty-two respectively.

The World's Most Popular Group

"Sure, we can be cocky and say we'll last

ten years or something, but we're lucky

if we last ten months."

—*John Lennon, 1963*

It was clear by the beginning of 1964 that "Beatlemania" would not remain contained in Britain or the UK. The level of the group's popularity, combined with the astonishing speed with which they had risen to the top, made touring the world a must.

By February 1, "I Want to Hold Your Hand" topped the U.S. music charts. Only days later, the U.S. release of *Beatles Second Album*, which featured "I Want to Hold Your Hand," was met with unprecedented sales. On February 7, when the four lads stepped down off their plane at JFK airport in New York, they were greeted with nothing short of mass hysteria. (Even the Beatles could not believe the reception. As they taxied in, they assumed that someone like Elvis Presley or the president of the United States was arriving at the same time.)

Beatlemania became an official phenomenon in America on February 9, when more than 73 million people watched them perform on live television during the extremely popular *Ed Sullivan Show*. Less than four weeks later, the Beatles held the top five music singles in America simultaneously.

Now, more than ever, the group and its management felt the pressure to capitalize on their phenomenal success in as many ways as possible. To that end, the Beatles' first film, *A

Hard Day's Night, and its soundtrack album were released in July. The film was a first for many reasons, most notably because it was not only about the Beatles, but also a cynical commentary on what their lives were like as the world's most famous foursome. The accompanying album, too, represented something of a milestone. It was the first Beatles LP that contained only original material.

The pressure to sell themselves was quickly becoming an enormous strain for all involved. At one point in 1964, the Beatles played thirty-two concerts in nineteen days throughout Australia and New Zealand. All in all, they played before 200,000 fans during that time. Though they were gratified by the appreciation they received from their fans, the stresses and hassles of touring far outweighed that satisfaction. Increasingly, the group felt trapped. It seemed to them that their entire lives were spent traveling from a hotel to a show and back again.

John, perhaps more than any of the others, felt oppressed and angered by life on the road. In addition to the discomforts associated with being on tour, he also felt that the concerts they played were unfulfilling musically. Even more depressing to the band was the realization that all the screaming and chaos effectively drowned out their music in the arenas they played. It seemed, in fact, that the actual music was relatively unimportant to the fans.

"It's like we're four freaks being wheeled out to be seen, shake our hair about, and get back into our cage afterwards," John once complained. Paul, on the other hand, was happy with their immense popularity. He felt that the frenzied behavior of their fans was the ultimate approval, a love that came only with the greatest success. Of course, the stresses and strains of touring affected Paul significantly as well, but he was much more willing than the others to put up with the inconveniences in order to please his public.

The material on their next album, *Beatles for Sale* (known as *Beatles '65* in America), reflected John and Paul's unhappiness with life on the road and their growing dissatisfaction with the pitfalls of fame. (The title itself was an ironic comment on the crass commercialism of their lives.) Bleak, soulful songs with titles such as "I'm a Loser," "Baby's In Black," and "No Reply," spoke of depression, lack of self-confidence, and the insane frenzy of life in the spotlight. It had only been two years since their first big hits—only four years since they were all in school in Liverpool—and the Beatles were each millionaires and more famous than almost anyone in popular music history had ever been. John and Paul had achieved their boyhood dreams of making "lots of money" but that success came at a huge cost to them. In return, they had all but surrendered the rest of their youth and given up any hope of ever living a "normal" life.

The songs they included on *Rubber Soul*, released in 1965, took the moody, soulful nature of their previous album and embellished it with more sophisticated and interesting music. As always, they worked quickly in the studio. Although they recorded all the material in only a month, the album's sound is as good as similar records produced today that have taken many months, even years, to complete.

As always, both John and Paul were looking to expand themselves musically. To that end, John incorporated the sitar, in its first pop use, on his memorable "Norwegian Wood." A probable combination of fatigue from touring, fed by John's disenchantment with fame and fortune, made even Paul's writing during this period a bit more cynical. His songs, "You Won't See Me" and "I'm Looking Through You," both speak to the superficial nature of their celebrity and comment on how ridiculous the Beatles' popularity seemed.

The summer of 1965 continued to mark new achievements and distinctions for the group. In June, Buckingham Palace announced that the Beatles were to be made Members of the Order of the British Empire (M.B.E.s). Characteristically, John wanted to refuse the honor, feeling that it showed only too clearly that the Beatles had "sold out." Paul, of course, was absolutely

"It's like we're four freaks being wheeled out to be seen, shake our hair about, and get back in our cage afterwards," John once complained.

delighted with the recognition and openly took great pride in it.

In July, their second movie, *Help!*, and its accompanying album were released. Recorded in 1964 and originally called *Eight Arms to Hold You*, the music was good but, stylistically, was a move backward to an earlier point in the band's evolution. Still, some songs managed to break new ground. "I Feel Fine," for example—mostly a John composition—was the first recorded song ever to use feedback.

With the release of *Revolver* in 1966, the Beatles entered a new phase. Though the material was a logical progression from *Beatles for*

Ringo, John, Paul, and George show off their M.B.E.s after the ceremony in 1965.

Sale and *Rubber Soul*, the new album created a totally new sound. The lyrics and music were becoming even darker and more complex. By using a wide variety of classical instruments— with the brilliant help of George Martin—a new universe of moods and feelings could be evoked. Martin, who scored the cello on Paul's "Eleanor Rigby," was also the first to blend an entire classical orchestra with popular music.

As an artist, John also relied on George Martin to help him realize his musical goals. Influenced by various forces of the sixties— including psychedelia, marijuana, and Bob Dylan—John enlisted his producer to help him experiment with the alternative uses of studio technology. Songs such as "Tomorrow Never Knows" were the first in popular music to incorporate backward-running tapes, sitar music, and other distorted sounds. This bold, new "avant-garde" sound in Beatles music was one of John's most notable and impressive contributions to the group's sound. Many who knew him—including his ex-wife Cynthia—felt that 1965 and 1966 were the best songwriting years of John Lennon's life.

From the perspective of the Lennon-McCartney partnership, the songs of 1965 and 1966 were a perfect blend of both men at their peak of creativity. At the same time, however, each writer was also defining his own unique style. Back in Liverpool, their partnership had grown from a mutual love of music and as a way for each to bolster the other's insecurities. By 1965, however, each partner had gained confidence in himself and had developed a strong musical identity. The result was that they began to drift apart.

Though John and Paul were each evolving a more individual writing style, they still maintained a significant artistic influence on one another. The song, "We Can Work It Out," is a perfect example of the blending of this period. Paul's optimistic verse proposes patience, reconciliation, and compromise, while John's "fussing and fighting" bridge urges a solution because time is running out. Musically, Paul's melody is cheery and light. John's bridge, however, shifts gears abruptly into a minor key, adding a more foreboding feeling.

For each song written primarily by John— such as "Run for Your Life," in which the singer admits to being "a wicked guy" who was "born with a jealous mind"—there was a sweet Paul song like "Michelle" that featured his soft, sincere voice as he sang "I love you" and "I need you" in a clear and vulnerable style. Taken together, these different songs formed a unique balance of fun, cynicism, romance, and poetry. This kind of diversity kept their music both interesting and unpredictable. It also kept millions of Beatles fans around the world constantly wanting more.

By the summer of 1966, the strains and musical limitations of live touring had become too much for the band to bear. Intent on spending some personal time with their families and on other serious relationships, the Beatles decided to give up touring for good. On August 29, 1966, they performed their last live performance ever at Candlestick Park in San Francisco, California.

The Beatles were by now a worldwide institution. In fact, it was estimated at the time that there was a Beatles song being played on a radio somewhere in the world at any given moment of every day. The albums they had created so far had not only changed significantly in style from one to the other, but they had simultaneously changed the sound of popular music. And, as incredible as those achievements were, one thing is even more amazing: The best was still yet to come.

Chapter

The Studio Years

"We created an imagery of sound."

—*George Martin*

Heading into 1967, each of the Beatles had an estimated personal wealth of between $8 and $10 million. In addition, they had gained some other precious assets as well. The ability to enjoy privacy, freedom, and personal time was, for each of them, a much more valuable luxury than all their millions. Putting an end to the touring was both a welcome change and a great relief for all four men. After five frantic years of living, breathing, sleeping, and eating together, the Beatles now had the opportunity to grow more as individuals. They also had a chance to spend more time on their personal relationships—some with wives, others with girlfriends.

This time for personal growth enabled John to develop a close new relationship with a Japanese artist named Yoko Ono. While attending her show at the Indica Gallery in London on November 9, John met the avant-garde artist and was immediately drawn to her. Within weeks, they would be spending almost every waking moment together. This new relationship had an impact on many lives. It destroyed John's marriage, changed the course of his life, and effectively began the slow disintegration of his partnership with Paul.

Life without touring for the Beatles was by no means life without music. Unburdened by the rigors of life on the road, John and Paul both began to explore the infinite musical possibilities open to them in the studio. It was during this time that they began work on a "concept" album originally planned as a tribute to their Liverpool childhoods. With this in mind, John wrote "Strawberry Fields Forever," about a real place from his old neighborhood. Heavily influenced by avant-garde art and the emerging drug culture, John's song was a dreamy mix of weird sounds and a studio-enhanced tempo that gave it a characteristically dark and eerie quality. Paul's childhood remembrance came in the form of "Penny Lane." True to his usual approach, it was a cheery, charming song that offered nostalgic snapshots of everyday life remembered from his boyhood.

In February 1967, both "Strawberry Fields Forever" and "Penny Lane" were released as singles. They were also accompanied by an innovative product never before produced: Both songs were marketed with their own promotional films, which represented the first real "music videos" ever done. Dreamy, blurry, and surrealistic, these short films were visual interpretations of the songs.

On June 1, 1967, the Beatles once again created a landmark in the world of music and popular culture. It was on that day that *Sgt. Pepper's Lonely Hearts Club Band* was released. While it is true that their records up to this point had been significant and influential all around the world, this work was something entirely different—this was an album that became an icon of popular American tastes. It also changed pop music forever.

Almost immediately hailed as the Beatles' "masterpiece," the album created a tidal wave of interest, analysis, and discussion. Fans and critics alike sat and listened to it for hours, each time appreciating more the rich instrumentation, the complexity of the lyrics, and the uniqueness of the sound. Most albums that came before *Sgt. Pepper* had been a loosely tied together collection of complementary singles, often compiled by the producers and agents rather than the musicians. *Sgt. Pepper*, however, was a "total concept" album, even down to its graphic design. With their wild colors and psychedelic overtones, the cover and inside materials were "pure sixties." It was also the first album ever to have liner notes and printed lyrics. By packaging the album the way they did, the Beatles were the first music group to present rock 'n' roll music as an art form. Years after recording *Sgt. Pepper*, Paul recalled his thoughts and inspirations while developing the album:

Normally, a Beatles album would be just a collection of songs with a nice picture on the cover, nothing more. So the idea was to do a complete thing that you could make what you like of, just a little magical presentation.

Sgt. Pepper was the ultimate outcome of what was orginally conceived as the album about their childhoods. Instead of following that concept through, however, they wrote a series of highly imaginative songs about people, places, and visions in their minds. The songs are loosely connected by the idea that the Beatles (Sgt. Pepper's band) are performing these songs in front of an audience in the order in which they are played on the record.

Despite its immense success, the recording of *Sgt. Pepper* underlined the many personality and artistic differences that had been simmering between John and Paul. As the perfectionist, Paul would work on a song over and over again, constantly redoing it and trying it with different instruments. Working this meticulously on each composition often annoyed John and frustrated him. John's creative process was much quicker and less detailed. Once he wrote something down or got the first few takes recorded, he wanted to move on to the next idea. John could not tolerate lingering over a song for too long— he was too restless a creative personality. If it had been entirely up to John, *all* their records would have been recorded in eleven hours (like their first) and released the next day.

Also, John had always been convinced that Paul's songs received more finishing touches and, hence, more attention from George Martin, than his did. Looking back, Martin admitted that this was probably true, but only "because Paul was more interested." Paul, as Martin described it, would sit down before recording a song and ask detailed questions about what Martin was going to do with the instruments and the arrangements. They would go over Paul's songs carefully, almost note by note, trading ideas as the plan for the song evolved. John was less interested in such details. Before recording his songs, he would offer Martin a few vague ideas about what he wanted for feeling or sound, and he would expect his producer to come up with a way to achieve it. On *Revolver's* "Tomorrow Never Knows," for example, John told George Martin that he wanted the song to sound as if "the Dalai Lama was singing from a hilltop." On *Sgt. Pepper*, John explained that, for his song "Being for the Benefit of Mr. Kite!," he wanted a "fairground atmosphere" and that he wanted to get the feeling of "sawdust in the ring." "Can you do something about it?" he asked Martin in the studio.

George Martin has said that his primary job as a producer was helping the ideas that John and Paul had in their heads to become real. As he has explained it, he was often confronted with the challenge of creating an "imagery of sound...I'd then have to think how that imagery could be transformed into sound. The difference between John and Paul, fundamentally, was that Paul would want to know how I was going to go about achieving what he wanted. John couldn't care less. He just wanted the result."

Despite an evolving independence and the development of strong individual styles that strained the ties within the partnership, a few songs on *Sgt. Pepper* were still mostly collaborative efforts between John and Paul. "Getting Better" is one example—one where the distinctive elements of each songwriter can still be clearly seen. The optimistic concept of the tune is Paul's, but John contributed certain verses, such as, "I used to be cruel to my woman, I beat her and kept her apart from the things that she loved." In the chorus, Paul sings, "I've got to admit it's getting better, a little better all the time," to which John pessimistically added, "It can't get no worse" as a counterpoint.

Things, however, did get worse. On August 27, 1967, Brian Epstein was found dead in his apartment in London, the victim of a suicidal overdose. Though he had long been troubled by depression, it is most likely that despair over feeling obsolete as a manager was what finally overcame him. In many ways, he felt that, by 1967, his "boys" had gotten away from him. With the incredible reception to *Sgt. Pepper* and their already immense popularity, the Beatles no longer needed to have their image sold to the world. In addition, they were no longer touring. Epstein, understandably, felt as if his usefulness to the band was now over.

Epstein's death had a number of significant impacts on the dynamics of the group. In the past, he had been the force that had balanced all the egos, all the creative energy, and all the anxiety. Without him as their center, the Beatles—most importantly John and Paul—would be forced to fight out all their problems on their own. Of course, the loss of Epstein created new problems in itself. One of the biggest conflicts that would develop between John and Paul was Paul's attempt to fill in the management void that Epstein left behind.

In the wake of Eppy's death, Paul thought he should take more control and help the group stay on course. The others, however, resented Paul's bossiness. This friction grew more serious as the next few years wore on. Eventually, it would mushroom into a battle that drove the group apart and pitted Paul against his three bandmates. John realized the significance of Epstein's death at the time. Looking back, he later admitted that "the Beatles were finished when Eppy died. I knew, deep inside me, that that was it. Without him, we'd had it."

The months that followed Brian Epstein's death were a disorganized, desperate scramble as the Beatles tried to keep themselves on course. On December 26, the *Magical Mystery Tour* album and television program premiered on British television. A nonstructured, loosely conceptualized piece that paled in comparison

"The Beatles were finished when Eppy died," John said.

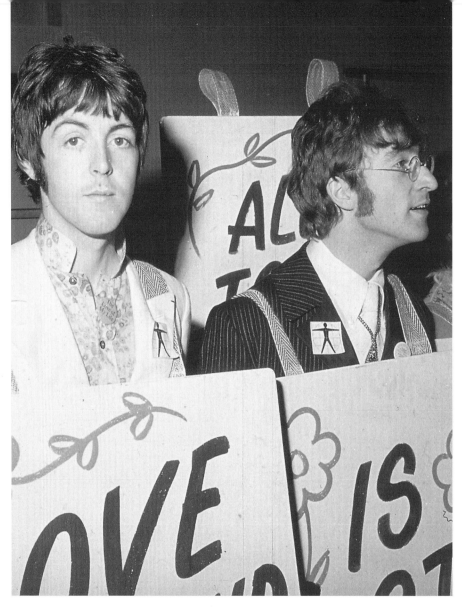

Paul and John promote peace and their album *Magical Mystery Tour* in 1967.

to *Sgt. Pepper*, the television show was essentially the Beatles' first public flop. It was no coincidence that it was also their first post-Epstein venture as well.

The failure of the *Magical Mystery Tour* project only fueled resentments in the band. Mostly Paul's brainchild, the project had never really interested John. In the wake of Epstein's death, however, he had agreed to go along with the idea in a vain attempt to keep the group together. The ultimate failure of the project was also a harsh reminder to the band of what happens when personal conflicts erode cooperation and the ability to work together as a team.

In May 1968, John and Paul appeared on *The Tonight Show* to officially announce the formation of Apple Corps. As they explained it, the company—financed by the Beatles—was conceived to offer new and promising artists a chance to be heard. The new company was also created partly as a response to Brian Epstein's death. In forming Apple, the Beatles felt as if they were at last taking control of their own business affairs. The complications and immense frustrations of business, however, would soon prove to be the most divisive factor in the group's eventual breakup.

By the time *The Beatles* (known popularly as the *White Album*) was released during the summer of 1968, the early stages of dissolution were already obvious. Originally called *A Doll's House*, the album's final title—essentially no title at all— clearly conveyed a sense that there was little "concept" or "unity" to this work. This was, in fact, true. The *White Album* was essentially a collection of individual songs, recorded at various times, and, in some cases, not even recorded with all four members together.

Various inter-group tensions were at the root of this disunity. Some resentments developed over the fact that John insisted on having Yoko in the studio during all of his work, an indulgence that broke one of the group's cardinal rules about keeping wives and girlfriends out of the recording process. Not only was Yoko there all the time, she even sang on John's "Bungalow Bill" and "Revolution #9." The latter was an avant-garde "art piece," directly inspired by Yoko's work, and notably non-Beatlesque.

Given the seamless fluidity and originality of *Sgt. Pepper*, the *White Album* was disorganized, rough, and unfocused. John, however, maintained that this was his favorite Beatles album, especially *because* it showed each of their identities separately. For John, who was the most unhappy just being "one of the four," this chance to assert his own vision was satisfying. Interestingly, included in the stark-white packaging of the *White Album*, were four separate photo portraits of the band members instead of one group portrait. Though this gave a subtle message, it was by no means insignificant. For the first time in their careers, the Beatles were presenting themselves as four individuals and not as the collective "band."

By the summer of 1968, a host of personal and financial problems were also contributing to the tensions between band members. In August, Cynthia Lennon sued John for divorce, on grounds of adultery with Yoko. Paul and his fiancée, Jane Asher, were also in the process of ending their relationship after years together. Mounting financial and legal complications were starting to make Apple Corps a thorn in John and Paul's respective sides.

That August also saw the Apple label release its first single, "Hey Jude," which was a Paul tune through and through. As the biggest-selling Beatles single of all time, the song also broke new ground in that it was seven minutes long (previous singles were held under three). Written to comfort young Julian Lennon during his parents' divorce, the song was an inspirational message that also gave hope to Beatles fans eager to believe the group was starting to heal some of its wounds.

By late 1968, John and Yoko were inseparable. John became obsessed with Yoko's life, her art, and her vision of the world. He even announced that his name was now John Ono Lennon and insisted on using "JohnandYoko" as his official signature and identity. Every gesture that solidified the bond between John and Yoko, however, drove another wedge between John and Paul. As he matured, John had grown away from his dependence on Paul, but he had replaced it with a very powerful new dependence on Yoko.

The filming and recording for *Let It Be* began in January 1969. Contracted before many of the group's troubles had materialized, the entire project turned out to be a full-scale disaster. The idea behind the album was to get back to the group's rock 'n' roll roots by doing songs that were simple, uncluttered, and did not rely on lots of studio tricks or production. With this end in mind, they broke away from George Martin and asked American music legend Phil Spector to act as their producer.

Bickering and conflicts between individual personalities caused George and Ringo to walk out of a number of *Let It Be* recording sessions. Not helping the situation was the fact that Yoko was there at John's side every minute, which greatly annoyed Paul ("Get Back" was rumored to have been written about Yoko, who is referred to as "Jo Jo").

Despite the animosity, there was still some collaboration on the album. "I've Got A Feeling" was written by both Paul and John: Paul wrote the first half, John, the second half. "One After 909" was an old tune they wrote together in 1959 in Liverpool. This song was picked from the past in an effort to rekindle fond memories of their old days of simple rock 'n' roll and uncluttered partnership. "Two Of Us" also looks back tenderly on a trip John and Paul took through Europe just before their breakthrough, when they were together as the best of friends. When all the songs had been recorded and thousands of feet of film had been shot and edited, most all who saw the final product agreed that *Let It Be* was in trouble. After months of deliberation, the project was shelved indefinitely.

In March, Paul and New York rock photographer Linda Eastman were married in London. All the other Beatles were conspicuously absent from the ceremony. Eight days after Paul's wedding, John and Yoko were married during a seventy-minute visit to the island of Gibraltar before flying to Paris. The fact that neither John nor Paul attended each other's weddings was no mere mistake of planning. Both men, from this point forward, were making it clear that they each officially had new partners. With these new partners came new directions, new aspirations, new identities, and a new independence that no longer fit with the demands of the Beatles.

From 1969 onward, business battles and personal conflicts caused the group to dissolve at an increasingly rapid rate. In May, John, George, and Ringo signed a business management contract with Allen Klein. Paul, however, refused to do so. He had fought to have Linda's father, Lee Eastman, manage the group. This was a point on which the others refused to concede. For Paul, it effectively marked the end of his time as a Beatle.

On July 4, John made a pointed personal statement by releasing his first solo single, entitled "Give Peace A Chance." Instead of

From 1969 onward, business battles and personal conflicts caused the group to dissolve at a rapid rate.

John and Yoko staged a "bed-in" for peace in 1969. They are shown here with friend Eamonn Andrews.

crediting Lennon-McCartney, John credited the
song to the "Plastic Ono Band."

In September, John and Paul lost legal control of Northern Songs, which owned the rights
to all Lennon-McCartney compositions. Because
of tax complications and debts, the rights became the property of ATV Music, headed by
British music mogul, Lew Grade. Fueled by
mounting frustrations and horrendous business
complications, the intense bickering and fighting
between John and Paul now grew to massive
proportions. Things that would have been small
arguments in years previous now turned into
violent and bitter confrontations between them.

Toward the end of 1969, *Abbey Road* was
released. Originally titled *Everest*, it was designed
with no title and no name on its front. The
cover was simply a photo of the four of them
walking across a street, each dressed in a highly
individual way. The fact that this album had no
official title or markings on its front was a testament not only to the Beatles' popularity and
power but also to the fact that there was little
unifying the band at this point. Though they
were back together with George Martin for this
final project, there was little he could do to
make the Beatles seem whole again. Martin has
described the album's material as two distinct
sides, each one a series of separate songs. Side
one, as he saw it, was rock 'n' roll in nature
but marked by distinct compositions from

songwriters who had well-developed identities. Side two was more of a "running series," containing two of George Harrison's finest tunes and a good deal more studio enhancement. George Martin later said that the more straightforward rock 'n' roll side of the album was "basically to please John" and the more heavily produced, studio-flavored songs on side two were "to please Paul."

Let It Be was finally released in March of 1970. Though it was recorded before *Abbey Road*, it would go down as the final installment in the Beatles amazing ten-year career. On April 10, Paul made the group's breakup official by publicly announcing his resignation from the Beatles. Seven days later, his first solo album, *McCartney*, was released. Unambiguously titled with the name of one single songwriter, Paul was making his break clear and tangible to his public. The almost instant success of the single "Maybe I'm Amazed" from that album enabled Paul to breathe something of a sigh of relief. It proved not only to him but also to all his fans around the world that life after the Beatles was not only possible, it could even be successful.

Sorting Through the Mess

"I've had two partners in my life, Paul

McCartney and Yoko.

That's not a bad record, is it?"

—*John Lennon*

ollowing not too far on the heels of Paul's solo debut, John released his first solo album with the Plastic Ono Band on December 11, 1970. In the years that followed, the creative competition that had privately fueled their partnership years before would now become a public spectacle. For every album or hit that Paul had, John would try to "answer" with one of his own. It was not long, however, before this public face-off turned into out-and-out nastiness, both in statements to the press and in thinly veiled attacks on one another that masqueraded as song lyrics.

By the end of December, Paul had begun proceedings in London's High Court to end the Beatles partnership. By March, he had won his case and all the group's business was ordered into the care of a receivership. The court order superseded any control that Allen Klein had and put all the group's affairs into the hands of a neutral, legal entity.

Although the business was now being handled by a neutral party, John, George, and Ringo felt anything but neutral about the way things were being done. In fact, while returning from court with George and Ringo after the court decision was handed down, John had his driver stop at Paul's house. John leaped out of the car, picked up a brick, and unceremoniously flung it through Paul's downstairs window. As the glass shattered, he threw a second brick, smashing another window. When Paul came out to see what was going on, he literally froze in shock. He could not believe that the person he used to call his best friend was behaving in such a horrible and violent way. The intensity of the fighting and acrimony, however, only continued to worsen as time went on.

On October 8, 1971, John released what would forever be known as his "signature" solo album: *Imagine*. Though the album's material was somewhat uneven, the title track became an instant hit and spoke eloquently to the essence of who John Lennon was, both as a songwriter and as a man.

The nine years that followed were a personal and creative roller coaster for both John and Paul. During this period, filled with a sobering mixture of failures and great successes, their careers were often forced to take a back seat to family life and personal goals. On their records, both men devoted many tracks to experimenting with different musical styles, trying always to further define their solo identities. They also spent a good deal of time trading insults and mocking one another through song. John ultimately stooped to a more intensive mudslinging campaign, most notably on *Imagine* with a song called "How Do You Sleep?," which included the lines:

The only thing you done was Yesterday
And since you've gone you're just
    Another Day
How do you sleep?

In response to John's jibes, some of Paul's
songs, like "Too Many People" and "Back Seat
of My Car" were not-too-subtle cuts at John
and Yoko's arrogance.

As the 1970s and 1980s wore on, Paul
achieved greater and greater superstardom as a
pop solo phenomenon. During much of that
time, he collaborated with ex-Moody Blues
guitarist Denny Laine in a songwriting partnership that was second only to that which he had
with John Lennon. For more than ten years,
Laine and McCartney worked together on songs
for their band called Wings. Though the backup
band changed constantly, the Laine-McCartney
years managed to produce dozens of chart-
toppers: "Uncle Albert/Admiral Halsey," "Jet,"
"Band On the Run," "Live and Let Die," "Silly
Love Songs," and "My Love," to name only a
few hit tunes.

In 1980, after spending many years in relative
seclusion as a "house husband" and family man,
John re-entered the pop music scene with the
album *Double Fantasy*. After its release on
November 11, the album did very well on the
music charts, particularly the single "Starting
Over," which also carried the clear message of
the album.

Less than a month after *Double Fantasy*'s release, on December 8, 1980, John's rejuvenated career was abruptly ended. That night, while walking into his apartment complex in New York City, John was shot dead by Mark David Chapman, a crazed fan. John had turned forty only two months earlier.

Though he was deeply hurt by John's death, Paul continued to take an active role in maintaining his status as the reigning king of pop music. In 1990, with his latest band, he finished a massive world tour that catapulted him back into the music limelight. Sold out in every city on the tour, Paul's show incorporated new material along with many old Beatle songs—some of which had never before been performed for a live audience.

Since the world tour, Paul has remained active by writing, recording new albums, making appearances on MTV, and exploring a number of other musical forums. In 1992, he impressed the entertainment world by successfully moving into the area of classical music. Working with collaborator Carl Davis, Paul composed a moving piece called the *Liverpool Oratorio*. Overall, the work was well-received by music critics and audiences in many countries. Paul, who finally had the opportunity to fully utilize his love of classical instruments and composition, created the work as a tribute to his childhood days in Liverpool.

In 1980, John was killed by a crazed fan in New York City.

Today, Paul
remains one of the
most powerful and
influential figures
in popular music.

A Look Back

"I'll tell you one thing, man. I'll never fall

out with anyone again in my life for that

amount of time and face the

possibility of them dying before

I get a chance to square it with them."

—*Paul McCartney*

Today, Paul McCartney admits that one of the greatest regrets of his life has been letting the bitterness between him and John remain unresolved for so long. Because of their inability to forgive each other, John's death left an enduring scar on Paul McCartney. It has also shown him—and others who know him—that despite all the bickering and nastiness, the two old partners had a love for one another that went deeper than any of their business conflicts or ego battles.

On his popular album *Tug of War*, Paul included a special song to John, entitled "Here Today," which spoke poignantly of his abiding affection for his childhood friend. That song, public statements, and special mention of John in his 1990 world tour, have all been genuine attempts to work through some of the pain and regret Paul feels.

Since Paul and John formally ended their partnership in 1970, Paul has co-written and performed with many other musical greats, including Stevie Wonder, Elvis Costello, Carl Perkins, and Michael Jackson. (It was Jackson who, incidentally, bought the rights to all Beatles songs for $47.5 million in 1985—Paul and Yoko together had offered only $21 million.) Despite his great commercial success, Paul has felt some-what unfulfilled artistically in recent years.

In addressing this point, he has said that he really misses the spark John offered him and the time they spent working together.

The vast majority of musicians whom Paul has worked with over the years—mostly those in his 1970s group, Wings—have ended up walking out on him because of his oppressive need for control. They have complained that Paul allows little room for the creativity of others and becomes "bossy" when his backup musicians are not giving him what he wants. While working with John, however, Paul was up against a true equal in a partnership that they both depended on for survival. Without John's constant input as a creative balancing force, Paul has lost a certain perspective on himself and his music. He has also lost a crucial source of honest feedback and useful criticism.

The evolution of Paul McCartney's music since the 1970s—without John—shows clearly the most important aspect of a great partnership: It is much more than just two people working together. A great collaboration is the product of many complex ingredients—both known and unknown—that combine in such a way as to create something greater. Even though personality, talent, and external circumstances all contribute greatly to the final outcome, it is the serendipitous and magical blending of these ingredients that, in the end, creates a truly brilliant partnership.

Further Reading

Baird, Julia, and Giuliano, Geoffrey. *John Lennon, My Brother.* New York: Henry Holt and Company, 1988.

Brown, Peter, and Gaines, Steven. *The Love You Make: An Insider's Story of the Beatles.* New York: McGraw-Hill Book Company, 1983.

Coleman, Ray. *Lennon: The Definitive Biography.* New York: Harper Collins, 1992.

Corbin, Carol L. *John Lennon.* New York: Watts, 1992.

Epstein, Brian. *Beatles: A Cellarful of Noise.* New York: Pyramid Books, 1964.

Gambaccini, Paul. *Paul McCartney: In His Own Words.* New York and London: Flash Books, 1976.

Giuliano, Geoffrey. *The Beatles: A Celebration.* New York: St. Martin's Press, 1986.

_____. *Blackbird: The Life and Times of Paul McCartney.* New York: Plume, 1992.

Harry, Bill. *The Beatles Who's Who.* New York: Delilah Books, 1982.

Lewisohn, Mark. *The Beatles Live!* New York: Henry Holt and Company, 1986.

Loewen, L. *The Beatles.* Vero Beach, FL: Rourke, 1989.

Bibliography

Brautigan, Richard. *The Beatles Lyrics Illustrated.* New York: Dell, 1974.

Coleman, Ray. *Lennon.* New York: Harper, 1985.

Davies, Hunter. *The Beatles: The Authorized Biography.* New York: McGraw-Hill, 1984.

Epstein, Brian. *A Cellarful of Noise.* New York: Pyramid, 1964.

Giuliano, Geoffrey. *Blackbird: The Life and Times of Paul McCartney.* New York: Plume, 1992.

————. *The Beatles: A Celebration.* New York: St. Martin's Press, 1986.

Shotten, Pete, and Nicholas Schaffner. *John Lennon in My Life.* New York: Stein and Day, 1983.

Williams, Allan, and William Marshall. *The Man Who Gave the Beatles Away.* New York: Macmillian, 1975.

Chronology

October 9, 1940 John Winston Lennon is born.

June 18, 1942 James Paul McCartney is born.

May 1957 Lennon puts together a skiffle group called the Quarry Men.

July 6, 1957 McCartney goes to a Quarry Men concert and meets John Lennon for the first time. He later becomes a member of the group.

February 28, 1958 After hearing the Quarry Men perform in Liverpool, George Harrison joins the band.

June 2, 1960 The group performs for the first time with a new name, the Beatles.

August 16, 1960 The Beatles travel to Hamburg, Germany, seeking fame and fortune. Their first performance is at the Indra night club.

March 21, 1961 The Beatles debut at the Cavern club in Liverpool.

June 1961 A single that the Beatles do back up on, "My Bonnie," is released in Germany.

December 3, 1961 After hearing them perform, Brian Epstein offers to manage the Beatles.

January 24, 1962 The Beatles officially make Epstein their manager.

May 9, 1962 Epstein gets the Beatles a recording contract with Parlophone, a small division of E.M.I.

June 6, 1962 The Beatles have their first recording session in London at the Abbey Road studios.

August 16, 1962 Drummer Pete Best is fired.

August 18, 1962 Ringo Starr quits his band, Rory Storm and the Hurricanes, and becomes the group's new drummer.

September 4, 1962 The Beatles first single, "Love Me Do," is recorded.

October 5, 1962 "Love Me Do" is released.

February 11, 1963 The Beatles record their first album, spending only eleven hours in the studio.

February 22, 1963 A company called Northern Songs is formed; it would publish all new Lennon-McCartney songs.

March 2, 1963 The Beatles' second single, "Please Please Me," becomes the number one song on the *Melody Maker* chart.

December 27, 1963 The London *Times* call Lennon and McCartney "outstanding English composers of 1963."

February 7, 1964 The Beatles are greeted by screaming and adoring fans after their arrival at Kennedy Airport for the start of their U.S. tour.

February 9, 1964 About 73 million television viewers watch the group sing on the *Ed Sullivan Show*.

June 12, 1965 Buckingham Palace says it will make Lennon, McCartney, Harrison, and Starr Members of the Order of the British Empire (M.B.E.s).

August 29, 1966 Tired after three years of touring, the Beatles give their last live concert at Candlestick Park in San Francisco.

November 9, 1966 Lennon meets Yoko Ono for the first time after he sees her art exhibition at the Indica Gallery in London.

June 1, 1967 The album *Sgt. Pepper's Lonely Hearts Club Band* is released.

August 27, 1967 Brian Epstein is found dead at his home in London. The Beatles are in Bangor at the time.

May 15, 1968 Lennon and McCartney are guests on the *Tonight Show*. They announce the group's new business, Apple Corps.

February 3, 1969 Against McCartney's wishes, American show business lawyer Allen Klein is hired to handle the group's finances.

March 12, 1969 McCartney and New York photographer Linda Eastman are married.

March 20, 1969 Lennon and Yoko Ono are married in Gibraltar during a seventy-minute visit to the country.

May 8, 1969 Except for Paul, the Beatles sign a business contract with Klein.

April 10, 1970 McCartney quits the Beatles. Seven days later, he releases his first solo album, entitled *McCartney*.

May 13, 1970 The film "Let It Be" has its world premiere in New York. The group does not attend.

December 11, 1970 Lennon's first album without the Beatles, *Plastic Ono Band*, debuts.

December 31, 1970 McCartney goes to High Court in London to officially dissolve the Beatles.

June 1971 Paul McCartney forms his first solo group, called Wings.

October 8, 1971 Lennon's *Imagine* is released.

November 17, 1980 Lennon and Yoko Ono's album *Double Fantasy* debuts.

December 8, 1980 Lennon is assassinated outside of his New York home.

1990 McCartney completes a world tour with his newest band.

1992 *Liverpool Oratorio* debuts in Liverpool, McCartney's first full-length classical composition.

Index